By the author previously published books:

(Swe) EVOLUTIONENS idéer – en kort berättelse om varför, när och hur människan (av allt att döma) tog fel väg, ISBN: 978-1502322159, sidor: 272, format: 15.24 x 22.86 cm, numen publications, Malmö, 2011-2015.

EVOLUTIONARY ideas – A short story about why, when and how humans (by all accounts) took the wrong path, ISBN: 978-1502377050, pages: 256, format: 15.24 x 22.86 cm, numen publications, Malmö, Sweden 2011-2015.

(Swe) Är präststyre på väg tillbaka i Europa? ISBN: 978-1500654894 sidor: 96, format: 14.0 x 21.5 cm, numen publications, Malmö, 2014-2015.

From Rio to Quito - A nine weeks photo odyssey in South America, ISBN: 978-1494742942 sidor: 96, format: 20.32 x 25.4 cm, numen publications, Malmö, Sweden, 2014.

(Swe) Locktoner och Tankens Mutation – om godhet istället för religion, ISBN: 9652229563 sidor: 108, format: 21.0 x 14.8 cm, numen books, Malmö, 1999.

FEAR OF
GLOBALIZATION
Essay by Richard Conricus

The idea of writing this essay has been in my mind since 2005, when I returned to Sweden after living in the Middle East for 12 years. I discovered how influential leaders of opinion and politicians, eager to appear as righteous humanitarians, chose to ignore essential cultural differences between us Swedes and immigrants from non-European cultures. The consequences of this attitude have led to unnecessary confrontation, anxiety, distress and, moreover, the emergence of populist movements that play on people's narrow nationalism at the expense of their global responsibilities as human beings.

The populists oppose the idea that people can become closer to each other, arguing that there are hierarchical differences between peoples and that the influence of other cultures poses an imminent danger to ours. Paradoxically, these populists act in the same manner as the extremists they fear. Their suspicion of "the other" stops people integrating into the global community, which, in recent decades, has joined people together in an increasingly shared economy, culture, politics and environment.

Planet Earth can no longer continue to be a battleground for ruling ideas: local conflicts and interests increasingly threaten the entire world. Extremists and populists threaten parliamentary systems and humanist democratic governance. It really is the "clash of civilizations" that Samuel P. Huntington described in 1961, although in my opinion he is wrong about the main cause of the clash, which is the inability to understand "the other". It is not just a matter of ignorance, but rather of a sheer lack of ability to identify with the other. When there is dissonance between willingness and ability, the outcome is inevitable. The will may be strong, but if capability is absent, all efforts are fruitless.

I suggest that the question can be further refined: that it is not simply a struggle between civilizations, but a struggle between open and closed societies. Open society creates one kind of civilization and closed society another. Which one is better equipped to face the inevitable process of globalization, people with humanistic, democratic and tolerant ideals, or people from authoritarian societies based on the idea that there is only one truth? The answer, of course, is the former. But if so, why has it gone so wrong in Sweden and other Western countries? Enemies of globalization, with a background in racist ideology, are gaining momentum. In Sweden, for example, they have become the third largest political party – and this in a country whose people are generally considered open, moderate and capable of critical thinking.

How, then, can citizens respond in face of the fear of the unknown which extremists and populists exploit? What is it that limits the ability to understand, and instead creates anxiety about the other and the unknown?

The major culprit is, in my opinion, that remarkable phenomenon called political correctness, which creates a blinkered view in the media and among the established parties, further veiled by conciliatory rhetoric, a view which neglects decisive cultural differences. As a result, citizens are driven to look for other ways to express their grievances. This stands in contrast to the historically successful compliance with continental Europe's diverse cultures among the Swedish population. Swedish society has only benefited from immigrants from other European countries. They brought considerable knowledge with them, and made a decisive contribution to Sweden's current leading position in the global community. Come to that, a large majority of living Swedes count non-Swedes among their ancestors - after the Second World War genuine ethnic Swedes can only in be found well-isolated areas like on the island of Gotland). However, in the meeting with non-European cultures, this earlier success has not worked. Why?

It is my contention that the populists, whether left- or right-wing, whether elite or common, owe their gains to people's fear, ignorance, unwillingness and inability to understand non-secular cultures. During the 250 years of communal development, from the Enlightenment to today's humanism and democracy in the West, we have become unable to handle opposing ways of life. Philosophical giants like Hegel, Hume, Kant, Kierkegaard, Montesquieu, Nietzsche, Descartes, Rousseau, Schopenhauer and Voltaire have no or few equivalents in other cultures, the essential difference between them and the great philosophers of Judaism and Islam (for example, Spinoza, Maimonides and Buber among the former, El-Faradi, Ibn Sina and Ibn Rushd among the latter) being whether their thinking was based on pure reason or on a bedrock of faith.

The French philosopher Bernard-Henri Lévy[2] recently listed Muslim Enlightenment philosophers and pointed to the Afghan leader Massoud (1953-2001), Bosnian President Izetbegovic (1925-2003), Bangladeshi Sheikh Mujibur Rahman (1920-1975), Kurdish nationalists and the Sultan of Morocco (1909 -1961) as representatives of the Muslim Enlightenment. But the intellectual stature and influence of these politicians and warlords can not be compared to the European Enlightenment personalities named above.

In point of fact, it was largely the work of the great philosophers that put the West out of step with much of the rest of the world. The West's openness is in conflict with large parts of the world, which are governed by the opposite of openness. While Judaism and Christianity, since the Enlightenment, have generally distanced themselves from the dictatorship of God, *sharia* (Islamic canonized law) has not undergone the same process. Islamists can therefore feel safe in acting in accordance with Islamic decrees that are anything but sympathetic to dissidents.

There is also at least one additional dimension to the problem of transparency and secrecy towards the other. Muslims have - for political purposes - deliberately withheld Islamic decrees that could very well have opened up Islam's introversion, and dramatically changed its relationship to its fellow Semites, the Jews. Islamists ignore less inimicable messages concerning the children of Israel in the Qur'an[3]:

> "Those were the ones upon whom Allah bestowed favor from among the prophets of the descendants of Adam and of those We carried [in the ship] with Noah, and of the descendants of Abraham and Israel, and of those whom We guided and chose." (19:58).

> "And We did certainly give the Children of Israel the Scripture and judgement and prophet-

hood, and We provided them with good things
and preferred them over the worlds." (45:16).

The Qur'an also gives Israel the right to stay in the
land:

"And then we said to the Children of Israel,"And
We said after Pharaoh to the Children of Israel,
"Dwell in the land, and when there comes the
promise of the Hereafter, We will bring you forth
in [one] gathering." (17:104).

The Qur'an also emphasizes Israel's status as the
Chosen People:

"O Children of Israel, remember My favor that
I have bestowed upon you and that I preferred
you over the worlds." (2:47).

Why do influential Muslims not follow the above decrees? I have posed this question to both Sunni and
Shiite Muslims, but have not received deliberate answers. Instead, the answers I received usually suggested
ignorance of the biblical Jewish record, which is the basis of Islam. Political reluctance has thus replaced such
an option, though the material to spread this knowledge exists.

Closed civilization, especially when religion and
politics go hand in hand, is impervious to reform and
fights furiously against any step to reform and to adapt
to the global community. For example, the moderate
Mu'atazilites failed to gain influence in Islam. Being
able to refer to "God in Heaven" is, as the world has
painfully learned, fatal when religious beliefs are allowed to rule the political sphere, and guide the development of communities.

The Bible is, in my opinion, an experience-based codebook for human existence, with a specific criterion for inclusion, namely monotheism. This is the belief in an omnipotent God (Yahweh/Allah), whose basic design, therefore, is intolerant. When put in the hands of fundamentalists, it means direct danger of life to dissidents.

Religious freedom does not mean that we must unconditionally accept the dictatorship of God, whether it is called Judaism, Christianity or Islam. It is inconsistent with democratic values that the supporters of religious dictatorship and monotheism are allowed to agitate freely without criticism because of political correctness.

Why are religious ideologies considered above political ideologies, especially given that in many countries they are the same thing? To criticize dictatorship by God should be perceived as upholding democracy. It has nothing to do with either anti-Semitism or Islamophobia. Divine decrees must be questioned, like all axioms. They are, after all, penned by humans, to control the masses and correct the "mistakes" that evolution has spawned.

Western democratic peoples are simply unaware of what the professor of Islamic law at Qatar University, Abd Al-Hamid Al-Ansari says[4]:

"They [the secular West] do not believe in religious and spiritual motives. They adhere to materialistic standards.... Terrorism is based on an extremist ideology, which takes over minds susceptible to this type of ideology.... It requires an ideological mixture... An ideological mixture which you plant in his mind and which takes over his soul. The first step is to sow hatred, saying that the other is not worthy of living, that the other is an infidel, that the other is an enemy who wants to attack me, that the other is a secularist, who is trying to change our identity, to invade [our world], and to Westernize our women, that the other wants to lay snares for Islam. They always portray us as targets, as if there are enemies lying in wait for us. This rhetoric about a nation constantly under attack is how hatred begins. This is how you plant hatred in the soul of a child, who later becomes an extremist. We must let go of the culture of denial, and stop saying: "This is not something a Muslim would do." We need to pinpoint what instills hatred, extremism, and takfir, and then remove these things from the curricula, the mosques, and the media. We should open up to other cultures. Why can't we be like other nations? How come they educate their children properly, and discover and invent new things? How come it is only our children who turn to destruction instead of construction?".[4]

The US Republican Party's candidate for the 2016 presidential election, Donald Trump, is an example of how populists are exploiting a gap in people's minds and, thanks to his rhetorical skill. He succeeds in duping ordinary people. The problem becomes even greater when the elite, in the form of influential leaders of opinion and political leaders do not dare to name things by their right names. It is important to note that the Western elite is not able to free itself from the hegemony of the humanistic world view. And hence fails to understand the hegemonies of competing cultures. Based on humanistic values of understanding, tolerance, compassion, reconciliation and respect for the individual, the elite seeks understanding for the perpetrator, rather than for the victim. The most peculiar is that the "elite" is not able to transcend its Western hegemonia- humanistic world view and understand the competing cultures hegemonies. Based on humanistic values of understanding, tolerance, compassion, reconciliation and respect for the individual the "Elite" seeks sympathy for the victims rather than scrutinizing the conduct of the victimized opposite.

Democratic humanism has been defined as follows:

> "Humanism is a democratic and ethical lifestance which affirms that human beings have the right and responsibility to give meaning and shape to their own lives. It stands for the building of a more humane society through ethics based on human and other natural values in a spirit of reason and free inquiry through human capabilities. It is not theistic, and it does not accept supernatural views of reality"[5].

Its opposite - theocratic anti-humanism, or dictatorship by God's – has been defined as:

> "A form of government in which God or a deity is recognized as the supreme civil ruler, the God's or deity's laws being interpreted by the ecclesiastical authorities"[6].

Theocracies are basically anti-humanistic, because

God's decrees are above the individual, who has no intrinsic value, unless he worships the omnipotent God. Monotheism is no exception. Certainly there are decrees that can be interpreted as humanistic values, but they are all primarily dependent on blind devotion and demands of proselytes to kill in God's name:

> "Put every man his sword by his side, and go in and out from gate to gate throughout the camp, and slay every man his brother, and every man his companion, and every man his neighbour." (Exodus 32:27).[7]

The text then describes how pleased God is after that the Israelites murdered infidels. The Christian version of this comes with Jesus' words in Matthew 10:

> "Think not that I am come to send peace on earth: I came not to send peace, but a sword. For I am come to set a man at variance against his father, and the daughter against her mother, and the daughter in law against her mother in law. And a man's foes shall be they of his own household." (34-36).

In the Qur'an, this became:

> "And kill them wherever you overtake them and expel them from wherever they have expelled you, and fitnah is worse than killing." (2:191).

The Qur'an further describes how fear of Allah must be manifested:

> "It is He who sent His Messenger with guidance and the religion of truth to manifest it over all religion. And sufficient is Allah as Witness. (48:28). ... And give tidings to those who disbe-

lieve of a painful punishment. (9:3) Fight them until there is no [more] fitnah and [until] worship is [acknowledged to be] for Allah. (2:193). O you who have believed, do not take the Jews and the Christians as allies. They are [in fact] allies of one another. And whoever is an ally to them among you - then indeed, he is [one] of them." (5:51).

To discredit others is part and parcel of religious confrontation with other faiths. How else would their interpretation be able to survive? Every religion/ideology must extol itself and emphasize its own excellence at the expense of everyone else. However, the Qur'an is sometimes extreme in this respect, which is one of the reasons why fundamentalist movements, such as Daesh (I.S. or Islamic State is a misleading term, since both Iran and Saudia, among others, are Islamic states), have no qualms about killing dissidents – that is, anyone who do not consider fundamentalist Sunni Islam be the only true doctrine:

"It is He who sent His Messenger with guidance and the religion of truth to manifest it over all religion." (48:28).

Seven *hadiths* even proclaim that stones can talk and betrays hiding Jews:

"You [Muslims] will fight with the Jews till some of them will hide behind stones. The stones will [betray them] saying, 'O 'Abdullah [slave of Allah]! There is a Jew hiding behind me; so kill him.' " (Sahih al-Bukhari, Volume 4, Book 52, Number 176:).

Such wording underlies the horrible crimes that fanatical worshippers perpetrate around the world. They follow what is written to the letter, believing that to be judged as true believers they may not deviate from *sharia* Islam. This does not mean that all worshippers of monotheistic faiths follow such decrees; but they are indicative of all believers' view of their own version's superiority over all other monotheistic teachings (Judaism, Christianity, Islam). There is only one truth, and people should be prepared to fight to the death for this sole truth. Only when such decrees are removed from the teachings of monotheism, in my opinion, can the humanistic values of monotheistic beliefs be taken seriously.

Hence, when democratic humanism meets anti-humanist theocracy, a conflict arises. For theocrats, God's decrees are untouchable, whereas the humanist's regards such views as personal values which must be valued as highly as the humanist's own ideals. The result is that the humanist tries to understand and overcome opposition. The theocrat, on the other hand, perceives the humanist as utterly in error, because he does not submit to God, or marginalizes God to almost nonexistence.

The theocrat perceives the world as divided into black and white, for or against, good or evil, while the humanist sees the world in a variety of cultural shades on Life's palette.

The humanist's concept of consensus does not work in meetings with theocratic cultures. Refined and conceptional rhetoric is perceived as weakness by those who do not hold the same values. Plain language is the only path for understanding any message. An old proverb says that you should talk to farmers in the farmers' way, i.e., adapt the message to the recipient's ability to understand what you are talking about.

The problem is therefore a lack of understanding, by both sides, of the values that each group bases its existence on; secularism and theocracy. This does not mean that all Westerners are secular, or that all Muslim immigrants are deeply faithful. But - and this is most important - people brought up in theocratic communities and indoctrinated with theocratic ideas from infancy (perhaps even epi-genetically based) can not be won over by logical reasoning. Logic simply does not work as a bridging argument, because there are different perceptions of reality. The Westerner holds that logic as unassailable, the Muslim holds the same of belief.

After living for many years in the Middle East (West Asia) among different cultures, I have come to realize how strong the inherited social code and everyday rituals are. Seemingly hostile ethnic groups, such as Jewish refugees (who after World War II fled from North Africa and settled in Israel) and North African Muslim populations have crucial common living codes and views of the world. Clan and tribal thinking are still very dominant of both groups and usually religion-based. The nuclear and multi-generational family is the hub around which everything revolves. Through marriage, new members are welcomed in the community, but they must comply with applicable codes and everyday rituals.

Many non-European immigrants would like to join the secular life, but are hindered because of (possibly) inherited codes and strict family rules. Not infrequently, crucial conflicts, even in their most brutal form result in the murder (so-called honor killings) of those who want to leave the clan or, by their actions, question the clan codes. The honor murder of Fadime Sahindal by her father in Uppsala in 2002 was a wake-up call for many Swedes. This and similar murders, concern exclusively girls who rebel and question patriarchal values that do not allow women to choose partners by themselves. Fadime Sahindal had a Swedish boyfriend, and refused to marry the cousin chosen by her family.

Any suggestion of mitigation in the legal prosecution of such oppression gives the wrong signals to the perpetrators and others who hold their views. Forced and child marriages are against the laws and customs of Swedish society, and the appropriate laws must apply equally to all citizens.

The same must apply to female circumcision. Mutilation of girls' genitals is disgusting and completely unacceptable. The same applies to religious coercion. In Western society, religion belongs to the private domain and should have no place in public decision-making.

The state has clearly highlighted its stand against such manifestations, and has created "Kvinnofridslinjen", run by the National Centre For Violence Against Women" on behalf of the government; yet girls are still exposed to genital mutilation and forced marriage. Religious police are also active and threaten those who do not follow the "divine decrees". In December, 2015, the Swedish Police listed 53 sites in Sweden where violent religious extremism is encouraged, a number which is growing, and parallel social structures also exist[8].

Why this indulgence?

Is it because Sweden wants to look good? As former Prime Minister Fredrik Reinfeldt said - just before his government lost its power in 2014:

> "I will appeal to the Swedish people to open their hearts to the very vulnerable people who we now see around the world ... Our assessment is that the immense ruthlessness in a broken world we see in our immediate vicinity is so serious that more people will be forced to flee to Europe and Sweden ... and I can already say that it will lead to great expense"[9].

We know what happened next. Proud of having been profiled as a humanitarian superpower, Sweden now appears to be rather a nation of naive, gullible, well-meaning but altogether unrealistic politicians and leaders of opinion. Pennants and cheers greeted many asylum seekers upon their arrival on Swedish soil. The Swedish Migration Board officially committed Sweden to unconditionally provide all Syrians arriving in Sweden with permanent residence.[10] Tens of thousands of Syrians relied on the promise of the Migration Board and, sometimes under inhumane conditions, put their lives at risk to reach Sweden. However, the present government, under Prime Minister Löfven, with the fence on the border with Denmark, put a definite stop for Sweden as a humanitarian superpower (4th Jan, 2016).

Compared with other countries, Sweden, in proportion to its population, has made an impressive effort for people in need. In 2015, Sweden accepted 198,246 asylum seekers, testifying to wholehearted acceptance of Sweden's refugee policy. The fact that approximately 80,000 of them were provisionally rejected only proves that the country's commitment to its humanitarian reputation was too great.

What about other countries? Is there any country in modern history that has received as many or more than Sweden has taken in? Yes, Israel is one: it managed to integrate almost a million former Soviet citizens between 1989 and 2006. Most were Jews, but this number also includes non-Jewish spouses and Christians. In 1989, Israel had a population of 4.5 million (half of Sweden's population in 2015), and in 2006, 7 million.

How could Israel succeed when Sweden fails?

The answer is, not surprisingly, that while Soviet Jews shared many cultural values with mainstream Israelis, together with a strong desire to be integrated, immigrants to Sweden in the 2010s come from radically different cultural backgrounds. In most cases they carry a theocratic mindset, and their norms of behavior are in often sharp conflict with Swedish values.

What cultural differences then, are there between Sweden and asylum seekers from Syria in 2015 (55 115 applicants), Iraq (21,955) and Afghanistan (65 044)? [11]

Before discussing these differences, it is it is worth considering how the present-day Middle Eastern states were formed, and what constitutes their ideological basis. As long as 100 years ago, David Fromkin wrote in his book "A Peace to End All Peace[12]," that it took 14 centuries for Europe to achieve stability after the Roman Empire, and warned that the post-Ottoman Empire could not be built in a day.

Totally insensitive to local conditions and the diversity of different ethnic groups, a still imperialist English and French governments approved the Sykes-Picot Agreement of 1916, dividing the Middle East in English and French spheres of influence. None of the current Middle East countries had yet been created. Contemporary demographic statistics show how ancient tribal and clan affiliations were ignored, and boundaries were drawn between populations according to totally alien considerations. The following illustration is a descriptive map of the actual social, cultural and ethnic relations in the early 1900s. The Sykes-Picot division and the modern borders of Israel are also inserted. It is reasonable to assume that if the split had occurred according to "ethnic borders", conflict in the Middle Eastern would have been dramatically reduced.

The "national" borders drawn by the Sykes-Picot Agreement were unlike the organization of modern states. It created quasi-national states with centralized governments and a political hierarchy, in place of the weakness of nepotism and central control in the Ottoman Empire; but, as a result of European secularism, fatally ignored the importance of religious schisms and ethnic differences, which undermined any national unity. Moreover, it abolished the Ottoman millet system, which gave a measure of autonomy to ethnic or religious minorities. This autonomy was very limited, but it did enable these groups to maintain their identity within the empire, and thereby minimized the potential for revolt.

The following illustration is a descriptive map of the actual social, cultural and ethnic relations in the early 1900s. Inserted are also the modern borders of Israel and the Sykes-Picot division. It is reasonable to assume that if the split had occurred according to "ethnic borders" the Middle Eastern conflict regions would have been dramatically reduced.

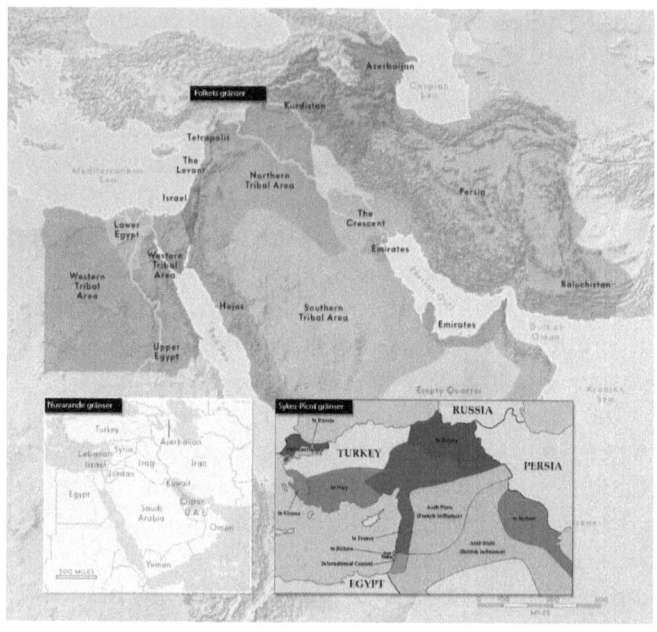

The pre-Islamic Arabic tribal constitution was built around a decentralized regional organization and self-sufficiency. The nomadic family structure was based on the number of children and livestock. Many children meant that more work could be carried out, meaning that more cattle could be reared, which led to greater prosperity and local influence. The relationship between families was based on a pattern of mutual recognition of physical power. Large families (clans) with many fighting men conquered neighboring families, seizing people, livestock and domains. Regional enclaves controlled by local chiefs maintained the balance of power amongst themselves to a greater or lesser degree, but united when subjected to threats from other regions.

The structure could be likened to the Russian doll, "Babushka": small independent units were enclosed in a larger unit which, in turn, was part of an even larger entity, until large, contiguous areas which had more in common than not, as regards language, religion, culture and economy, called themselves "nations".

This structure was understood by Muhammad, but he succeeded in uniting the tribes into a common front by introducing the idea of the Muslim community (the "*umma*") against everyone else. This concept became an even greater recipe for success through Muhammad's introduction of a higher power that required submission ("islam" means "submission"). Attacks against infidels were religiously sanctioned, even a requirement. Muhammad introduced the concept of the confrontation between "dar al-Islam" ("the Islamic world/region", meaning Muslim countries at peace with one another) and "dar al-harb", ("the war world/region", meaning infidel countries). These changes played out against the background of a war-weary Europe, with the Byzantine Empire in dissolution after the terrible Justinian Plague, which broke out in Constantinople in 541, leading to the death of about 30-50 million people. This event decimated the armies that were to meet the Muslim invasion forces, which largely escaped the plague, owing to their isolation from the plague in Byzantium.

The concept of *jihad* (holy war, though the word literally meant only "struggle"), which in the Qur'anic original is expressed solely in the context of defence against attacks on; or oppression of Islam, began to broaden. In the theological debates of early Islam, it became tantamount to aggressive holy war against all infidels. The

Byzantine and Persian empires both fell, and for 500 years the Islamic Empire continued to spread, including the invasion of the vastness of India which, according to the Belgian orientalist Koenraad Elst, resulted in the death of nearly 80 million Hindus. [13]

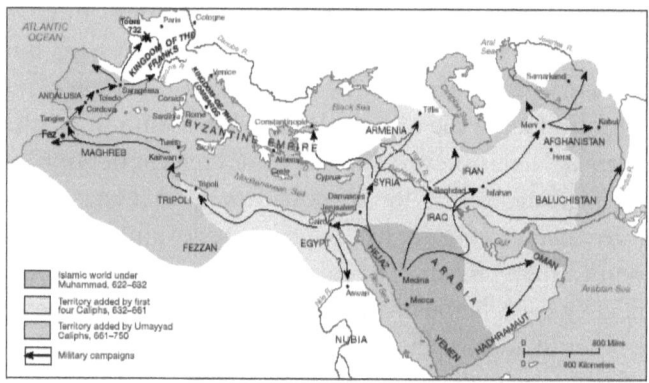

In 661 CE, the first caliphate dynasty was founded, with Damascus as its capital. Muslim armies had then conquered the Middle East, North Africa and penetrated all the way to the Indian border. Muhammad's strategy had succeeded. Arab clan and tribal communities were united under the flag of Islam. The new religion successfully grafted Arab custom and identity on to the scion of Judeo-Christian roots.

It was still to reach its final form, however, as we shall see. Continued conquests and increasing urbanization demanded amplification of Qur'anic precepts and their adaptation to non-Bedouin peoples. Furthermore, schisms had already begun to appear. Doctrinal differences grew early on out of the struggle for the succession to the caliphate, beginning with the revolt of the

Khawarij, on the one hand, and the establishment of the Shi'a, on the other. Nonetheless, the cultural basis of Islam was firmly established.

Muhammad's strategy has developed in our time into the ideological basis of Da'esh, with its barbaric rampage in today's Middle East, and with ramifications far into secular Europe and other Western countries. The claim that Da'esh (IS) does not represent Islam is totally wrong. In fact, Daesh follows Muhammad's strategy to unite all Muslims in a new caliphate. A further complication of coexistence with other faiths lies in the fact that Islam has for centuries outlawed any attempts at reformation. On the contrary, as one of999 Islam's most important Western scholars, Hamza Yusuf (himself a convert), claimed during a presentation in 2010 "Rethinking Islam reform":

> "A reformed Islam is not Islam, because Islam from the outset is reformed [derived from Judaism and Christianity]". [14]

Yusuf believes that Islam at most can allow "renovation" of the doctrines.

This means that Islamic reform movements that preach obedience to the European system of laws rather than obedience to sharia are considered heretic. Islam's most extreme and most fundamentalist practitioners, Da'esh, has, over recent years shown countless samples of how infidels will be treated. The doctrines of Da'esh attract not only Sunni Muslims in Iraq and Syria, but also Muslims from the rest of the world. Even Swedish citizens have succumbed to them, which casts a scathing light on Swedish politicians, whose constitutional obligation is to foster and safeguard democratic ideals for all citizens, regardless of religious affiliation.

Islam today has 1.5 billion worshippers. They are mainly located in tropical, sub-tropical, desert and steppe countries, but Islam and fundamental Islamism exist in Sweden too. Gothenburg is singled out as one of primary recruiting bases of Da'esh in Europe. – "A pantry full of cannon fodder to IS", says Ulf Boström, officer of the integration department of the police in Gothenburg[15].

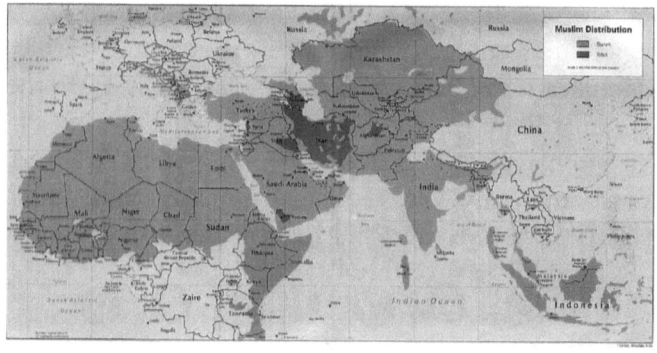

SÄPO has documented 130 cases from Gothenburg, but argues that the real number is much higher.

What then, motivates Muslims brought up in Sweden to join Da'esh?

The difference between Muslims and the vast majority of other Swedes lies in the cultural codes that Islamists bring to Sweden or any other country. An authoritarian upbringing in theocratic societies confers a different outlook on life. When intolerance of dissent for the Swedish democratic system and humanist ethical codes are nourished in favor of Islamic hegemony, the individual young Muslim becomes alienated and destined to turn to movements like Da'esh. An evolutionary process brings youthful transparency into conflict with the more rational constitution of mature brains. This dichotomy is controlled by the brain's limbic system, which controls emotional experiences and the prefrontal cortex, which is responsible for rational thinking. At a young age, and especially between the years 13-25 the limbic system is vastly more active than the prefrontal cortex, says Yossi Chalamish[17,] brain scientist at the Weizmann Institute in Israel. Emotions dominate young brains. Only at maturity is a balance is achieved between the emotional and the rational areas of the brain. Chalamish compares knife attacks by individual Muslims in Israel against Jews and Da'esh barbarism in Syria in Iraq: both are the result of the elimination of the influence of the prefrontal cortex. Emotions have taken over rational thinking, Chalamish claims.

Leaders of all sorts, dictators, democrats, anarchists, etc. exploit this evolutionary phenomen to enthuse companions and spread ideas. Problems arise when a leader - whether for religious or outright psychotic reasons – aims to block the directives of the prefrontal cortex, allowing the limbic system to take over. This happens when normative behavior is replaced by blind obedience to a ruler's will or the dictates of religion.

Hence, divine decree must be questioned, as has been said above. Fanatics are hard to reach and harder to persuade, which is why counter-measures should focus on informing ordinary people, so that they turn away from the agitators and instead affirm the messages of love, peaceful coexistence and respect for each person's religious affiliation that can also be found in the Bible and the Qur'an.

None of the figureheads of monotheism (Abraham,

Jesus and Muhammad) have made a self-recorded text: the whole idea of divine decree rather involves later recensions of the ideas of rhetorically gifted people as to about how life and society could be improved. These ideas found favor with the masses because they were presented at the right time and in the right context. Reform movements have subsequently adapted the doctrines to the current Zeitgeist and, moreover, since the Enlightenment have struggled to separate the state from the church - except in Islam.

In countries such as Sweden, Denmark, Britain, Holland, France, Germany and Norway motions are heard for the introduction of Muslim enclaves governed by *sharia* law: a notion that violates everything the West since the Enlightenment has achieved in neutralizing domination by the Church.

To prevent this development, the EU must implement a consistent information campaign, with the aim of teaching immigrants about what responsible freedom means, informing them about the dividing line between personal faith and civil governance, that religious dogma has no place in the political process and, not least, tolerance of dissent and the meaning of religious freedom.

A video that should trigger alarm bells shows how Sunni Muslims in Norway unanimously support the stoning of erring women. In this 2013 video from Islam Net, its chairman, Fahad Ullah Qureshi, during a panel discussion on "Islam in the media" asks the 4,000 Muslims gathered:

> "How many of you agree with the punishment described in the Qur'an and the Sunna, whether it is death, whether it is stoning for adultery,

whatever it is? If it comes from Allah or his messenger, it's the best punishment for humanity and it should apply in the world? Who is for it?". [17]

The video shows that all raise their hands, causing the chairman to come up with the following question:

"Allahu akbar, are you all extremists? ... So all of you say you are ordinary Muslims .... and that all of you go to normal Sunni mosques? ... What do the politicians say now? ... What will the media say now? Allahu akbar! ... They have to tell us all to leave this country [Norway]". [ibid]

The cultural differences between Swedes/Swedish society and asylum seekers from Afghanistan, Syria and Iraq is thus enormous. I am obviously not referring to the moderate Arabs, Kurds and Yazidis seeking asylum in Sweden, but to the traditionally trained and obedient asylum seekers. Even the more secular-minded among them involuntarily and intuitively bears codes reflexively governing their daily lives, in the same way as Swedes are controlled by codes and act in a normative Swedish way. Differences in perception of the world probably can not be greater than between a Swedish girl raised in the West Harbour (Västra hamnen) in Malmö and a boy from the Helmand province in Afghanistan. She lives on the shoreline of the Öresund Strait, in a part of Malmö where internationally renowned property developers and architects have created a paragon of sustainable living and working conditions. The boy comes from a mostly tribal and rural society where only about 3% of the households have clean drinking water and about 33% of the roads are not passable during certain seasons and in some areas there are no roads at all.

What then is the world view of asylum seekers from Afghanistan, Syria and Iraq when they arrive in Sweden?

Perhaps one of the main differences is the latter's adherence to sharia law. Around 800 million Muslims want to live under sharia law or can be said to be heavily radicalized by it. [18]

Christian Protestant doctrine has no corresponding law because the Church of Christ, according to Martin Luther, was not intended to be a church of laws, but a personal spiritual law to be held in the spirit and visible by good deeds. [19]

Why then does Islam have its religious law? Islam is, after all monotheistic. The answer is that Islam is founded on a mother religion, Judaism, which requires a religious law, *halacha*. Protestantism, however, breaks away from one of the pillars of monotheism by basically having only the Ten Commandments as a guiding code. How then is Protestantism articulated without the presence of religious law which basically control every believer's waking moment?

First, some general observations are due, regarding Christianity's historical significance in the development of modern society. The development of Christianity is chronologically related to the development of Europe, from the Reformation (the birth of Protestantism) and the Enlightenment to modern society. Protestantism is the mother of our governance, and its part in the definition of democracy is not as odd as that first may seem. All social entities, from the beginning of civilization, are based on a conceptual model of a world ruled by gods or God.

The Reformation led to a revaluation of the Bible and Judaism's rabbinical texts which, in turn, were based on even older heritages, namely the first civilizations of Mesopotamia - Sumer and Akkad - and Zoroastrianism (Persia/Iran).

For example, up to the Enlightenment there was a debate about whether God required a monarch to lead a country (such as the kingdoms of Israel and Judah), or if in fact it was the case that God punished the Israelites by allowing a secular monarch (an institution which often resulted in cruel and despotic rulers, as in all other countries and times) because of people's deviation from true belief in a God.

A discussion that was concluded by the Enlightenment was its demand to separate Church and State. Such a move rests on the conclusion that Man has constructed a higher power which - being a construct - does not know what it knows about the knowledge it created (see below for a more challenging definition*). This may sound convoluted, but not more so than the endless meanderings of the evolving human concept of a Divinity.

Enlightenment philosophers wanted to persuade mankind to think outside the framework of a single divine truth, which rulers had hitherto used to control, govern and oppress people.

A supreme entity of cognizance which itself is incognizant, of what the incognizants' cognizance comprehend about the incognizant that the cognizance has created.

This is, among other things, the heritage of the girl from the West Harbour in Malmö. Her ancestors had fought for freedom from the Church's supremacy. They had fought for the right of girls to education, women's suffrage, equality and the right to their own bodies. The boy from Helmand Province in Afghanistan carries an entirely opposite heritage when he seeks asylum as an unaccompanied child in Sweden. An infinite amount of work is required for the girl and the boy to be able to coexist on the girl's ethos. The next question, then, is where the line should be drawn before the boy completely loses his identity and thereby loses his footing in a secular world.

Perhaps the answer is not that complicated. Is it enough to follow the Golden Rule that is already represented in all the world's religions and cultures? That is, to treat one's neighbor as you yourself want to be treated, to open opportunities for respect, dialogue and intangible exchanges.

The question is whether the Afghani boy has both the will and the ability to break these very real barriers and seek integration into Swedish society, and whether the Swedish girl wants to help a person in need.

Is it possible to merge the two cultures without two human identities being lost?

Afghanistan is an Islamic republic based on sharia law. The Afghan constitution declares Islam to be the country's law, with the support (according to the Pew Research Institute, 2013) of 99% of the population[18].

Syria is a country in dissolution with hundreds of thousands of dead, 6.6 million displaced within the country and 4.8 million refugees in neighboring Jordan, Lebanon, Turkey and Europe (2016). Syria is made up of a variety of ethnic groups and was, until the civil war, incontestably ruled with an iron fist by the Assad family. The Assad clan belongs to the Alawite community, and represents a minority of about 13% of the Syrian population. The Alawite faith is a variant of Shi'a Islam, with its religious center in Shiite Iran. Most of the Syrian population (74%) are Sunnis, who regard the Shi'a as heretics.

Iraq is also in dissolution, involved in overt or covert struggles between its three dominant groups, These are the Shiites (60%-65%), the Sunnis (32%-37%) and the Kurds; (70-75% of Kurds are Sunni Muslims and approximately 3-5% Shites). There are also an increasing number of worshipers of the ancient Persian religion of Zoroastrianism, which had major impacts on Monotheism mother religion Judaism. The Kurdish population also includes the ethnic group Yazidis, which Da'esh tried to erradicate by genocidal war and the exploitation of Yazidi women as sex slaves.

> "The Yazidis are a Kurdish religious minority that ISIS had long excoriated as "devil worshipers" and vowed to exterminate. Their Mount Sinjar heartland was in the far northwestern corner of Iraq and outside official K.R.G. territory, making them especially vulnerable. ... In Sinjar that day — Aug. 3 [2014] — ISIS began carrying out mass executions, a slaughter that would ultimately claim the lives of at least 5,000 Yazidis. They were also rounding up thousands of girls and women to be used as sex slaves."[20]

Iraq is controlled by a combination of civil and sharia law. Rule by sharia law is supported by 91% of the population, according to the Pew Research Institute (2013).

According to the institutes opinion poll, a majority of 58% of all Muslims in the world hold that *sharia* law should be the law of the countries in which they live, thus not only in Muslim countries.

What then is *Sharia*? Muslims believe that Allah, through Archangel Gabriel, appeared and revealed the Qur'an to Prophet Mohammed. As we have noted, the need for interpretation and amplification arose immediately, a need answered by hadiths. These which are a compilation of sayings of the Prophet, outside the formal Qur'an. The problem with the hadiths is that many have been deemed illegitimate: of the 600,000 hadiths analyzed, only 7,275 could be accommodated within the criteria set by El-Bukhari in his "*Sahih*" (= "genuine")[21], the most widely accepted of such compilations. He performed his work more than 200 years after Muhammad's death.

Hadiths are divided into their *mutznaf* (text) and their *isnad* (chain of communication). Now, since the text is always a direct quotation of the Prophet, it is not open to scrutiny, because the Prophet's words are sacrosanct, like the text of the Qur'an. This left only the isnad open to analysis, whether each link in the chain was plausible. Thus, the first person of the chain had to be a Companion of the Prophet, i.e., a contemporary who was with him, and the next in line a Follower of the Prophet, i.e., a member of the next generation. The question is whether this criterion were too imprecise, since it only requires a linear reference: who heard it from whom. It is probably not far-fetched to assume the possibility of someone who was familiar with this criterion being able to fabricate both mutznaf and isnad for his own purposes. In other words, the saying which was said to come from Muhammad, could in fact be the result of a personal agenda. An example of this is Umar Ibn al-Khattab's assertion that he heard Muhammad preach that all Jews and Christians should be expelled from Medina.

> "Its authenticity is debated. One of Umar's guides in Jerusalem was a Jew named Kaab al-Ahbar. Umar further allowed Jews to worship on the Temple Mount and the Wailing Wall, while the Byzantines banned them from such activities. Thus, the authenticity of the clause regarding Jews is in question."[22]

Different interpretations of hadiths are also one of the causes of the bloody conflict between Sunni and Shi'a Muslims. For example, there is disagreement about a *hadith* concerning temporary marriage, *mut'ah* (meaning joy or pleasure), making it possible to establish an agreement for the use of a woman over a certain period (prostitution - even for a short time as a single night). The Shi'a permits this under on the grounds that it is a genuine *hadith*; something that Sunna vehemently denies.

The third source of *sharia* law is the consensus of "the learned", namely, doctors of law in the various colleges that sprang up to study jurisprudence. As mentioned above, their authority to pronounce was considered to have come to an end several centuries ago by the Sunnis, though the Shi'a still accept the precepts of their Ayatollahs. A number of such schools of jurisprudence existed, and adherence to one particular school or another varies from place to place and sect to sect. Thus, the most severe school of law, the Hanbali school, is accepted by the dominant Sa'udi Wahhabi sect and those whom we call fundamentalists..

Sharia is therefore practiced differently in Muslim countries There is, however, agreement about 180 verses (out of 350) from the Qur'an, where the intention can be inferred unequivocally, without the risk of misinterpretation.

So, what are the rulings of *sharia*? I have chosen here to quote some of the laws that are repugnant to Western society:

> "The [unmarried] woman or [unmarried] man found guilty of sexual intercourse - lash each one of them with a hundred lashes, and do not be taken by pity for them in the religion of Allah , if you should believe in Allah and the Last Day. And let a group of the believers witness their punishment." (Qur'an 24:2).

A verse of stoning adulterers to death is not to be found in the Qur'an, but Muhammad's companion Umar (second Caliph, 634-644) left no doubt that this penalty was practiced during Muhammad's leadership. Sacred traditions and classical laws also confirm that it was so.

> "... So do not take from among them allies until they emigrate for the cause of Allah . But if they turn away, then seize them and kill them wherever you find them and take not from among them any ally or helper." (Qur'an 4:89).

"O you who have believed, indeed, intoxicants, gambling, [sacrificing on] stone alters [to other than Allah], and divining arrows are but defilement from the work of Satan, so avoid it that you may be successful." (Qur'an 5:90).

"And We ordained for them therein [Torah] a life for a life, an eye for an eye, a nose for a nose, an ear for an ear, a tooth for a tooth, and for wounds is legal retribution." (Qur'an 5:45).

"[As for] the thief, the male and the female, amputate their hands in recompense for what they committed as a deterrent [punishment] from Allah" (Qur'an 5:38).

"Indeed, the penalty for those who wage war against Allah and His Messenger and strive upon earth [to cause] corruption is none but that they be killed or crucified or that their hands and feet be cut off from opposite sides or that they be exiled from the land." (Qur'an 5:33).

Notably, the *sharia* law that homosexuals should be imprisoned, flogged or executed has no basis in the Qur'an. The only appropriate verse is as follows:

"Do you approach males among the worlds. And leave what your Lord has created for you as mates? But you are a people transgressing." (Qur'an 26:165-166).

It is strange, therefore, that Islamic countries impose very severe penalties for homosexuality.

On the other hand, the Qur'an - and hence sharia law - gives Muslim men the right to beat their wives:

"Men are in charge of women by [right of] what Allah has given one over the other and what they spend [for maintenance] from their wealth. So righteous women are devoutly obedient, guarding in [the husband's] absence what Allah would have them guard. But those [wives] from whom you fear arrogance - [first] advise them; [then if they persist], forsake them in bed; and [finally], strike them." (4:34).

Women are judged in the Koran to be less credible why it takes two women to each man's testimony:

"... And if there are not two men [available], then a man and two women from those whom you accept as witnesses - so that if one of the women errs, then the other can remind her. (2:282).

The requirement to wear face-covering veil is based on a (deliberate?) misinterpretation of a verse in the Qur'an:

"And when you ask [his wives] for something, ask them from behind a partition [hijab]" (Qur'an 33:53).

The call is then for men to be behind a curtain, not women to hide their faces. "Hijab" is used in the Qur'an as an expression of something that is different, and never in connection with women's dress code. Nowhere in the Qur'an does it explicitly that women should hide the head, face or hair. However, women are asked to dress modestly:

"And tell the believing women to reduce [some] of their vision and guard their private parts and not expose their adornment except that which [necessarily] appears thereof and to wrap [a por-

tion of] their headcovers over their chests ..."
(Qur'an 24:31).

A Muslim man can divorce his wife by saying three times "I divorce you". The corresponding option does not exist for women.

"Divorce is twice. Then, either keep [her] in an acceptable manner or release [her] with good treatment." (Qur'an 2:229).

A Muslim man can have up to four wives:

"... Marry of the women, who seem good to you, two or three or four" (Qur'an 4:3).

Marriages with minors is based on the Prophet Muhammad's engagement with Aisha when she was aged six, their marriage taking place when she was nine (Muhammad was 50 years of age). The Qur'an enumerates specific situations, among others that marrying girls who are not yet menstruating is considered allowed:

" ... and [also for] those who have not menstruated" (Qur'an 65:4).

What, then, says the West of *sharia* law? In 2003 the European Court declared that:

>"... a sharia-based regime was incompatible with the [European] Convention, in particular, as regards the rules of criminal law and procedure, the place given to women in the legal order and its interference in all spheres of private and public life in accordance with religious precepts."[23]

It must be admitted, however, that on the basis of the Bible's misogyny, women have been treated appallingly throughout history. Even in the West, the Magna Carta of 1215, for example – though admittedly its main aim was only to limit the king's power - reduced women to a mere appendages of their husbands:

> (1) "TO ALL FREE **MEN** OF OUR KING-DOM we have also granted, for us and our heirs for ever, all the liberties written out below, to have and to keep for them and their heirs, of us and our heirs."

> (54) "No one shall be arrested or imprisoned on the appeal of a woman for the death of any person except her husband."[24]

It was almost 600 years later, with the support of the Enlightenment, that the first groundbreaking lawsuit was brought against outmoded social codes. In her "A Vindication of the Rights of Woman" (1792)[25], Mary Wollstonecraft succeeded in raising contemporary attention in England to the appalling situation of women.

Wollstonecraft ventured to express ideas about equality in women and men: that girls and boys have equal cognitive abilities, and should therefore be given the same upbringing and education.

This is a completely obvious requirement for us who live in Western democracies, but still represents utopia for women in many parts of the world, even in this year of 2016.

This is the case, for example, in Saudi Arabia, which autocratically and rigorously still maintains the legacy of the Prophet Muhammad. According to "Polity IV

Individual Country Regime Trends, 1946-2010", Saudi Arabia and Qatar are the world's worst repressive regimes. Meanwhile, Saudi Arabia is America's main ally in a turbulent Arab world. Saudi Arabia is also Sweden's single most important trading partner in the Middle East. In 2014, exports to Sa'udi Arabia amounted to around SEK 11b. [26]

The nominating of Sa'udi Arabia as the most oppressive regime does not come from some obscure protest movement. Polity IV is CIA-funded and thus subordinate to the US government. Polity IV gives countries like the United States and Sweden its top rating of 10, while Saudi Arabia and Qatar get the lowest possible -10. By way of comparison, Brazil rated -9 in 1966, but 8 since 1989 8. [27]

The world's most oppressive country, Saudi Arabia – a practitioner of the extreme Wahhabi sect (also known as Salafi) - requires women to wear the "*abaya*" (full body clothing) and "*niqab*" (veil), gives women limited opportunities for education and career, prohibits women from driving, prohibits social contact with male non-family members. It is a mandatory requirement that a male family member or "patron" controls every form of personal activity, such as opening a bank account. [28]

In 2005, the recently deceased (2015) Saudi King Abdullah tried to reform Saudi Arabia, but he faced powerful opposition from the Wahhabis, primarily from his half brother, Crown Prince Nayef Bin Abdul Aziz and the dominant Saudi clergy, who have the power to intervene everywhere in society, through the *mutawiyin* (religious police), wherever and whenever they discover Saudis who do not obey orthodox Islam.

In January 2012, the King appointed a relatively reformist head of the religious police. For example it was now possible for women to work in special clothing stores for women, instead of earlier, when only men could be shop assistants. He also managed to push through a law that gave women the right to vote in the 2015 elections.

However, according to Saudi law, it is still allowed to marry off a 10-12 year old daughter after a contract has been concluded between the child's parents and a man.

But women's rights are also curtailed in the West, if to a lesser degree. Sweden was the last of the Nordic countries to give women suffrage rights, in 1921.

In the US constitution the rights of women were first mentioned in a supplement (Amendment 19, Women's Suffrage), which was ratified in 1920. [29]

> "The right of citizens of the United States to vote shall not be denied or abridged by the United States or by any State on account of sex.

This was introduced as a result of the successful struggle by the suffragette movement in the late 19th and especially the early 20th Century, claiming that women should also have the right to vote.

To us this is an obvious fundamental right in every society, regardless of government, yet, as we have seen, it is still to be implemented in all countries.

All the more surprising is that in fact that equal rights for women and men in the US are still not enshrined in the US Constitution.

Since 1982, there has been a deadlock on the legislation proposed, the Equal Rights Amendment, that would give women equal status with men before the law. The supplement was introduced in 1923 and approved by the US Congress, but was blocked because three states did not ratify it.

In 1972, Congress approved a proposal that had become three-quarters of the US states – as a result of changed criteria - had five years to ratify the amendment. This did not happen. Instead, in 1980, the Republican Party removed its support for the extension, which prompted Congress to extend the ratifying process further, to 1982.

The states that refused to ratify the extension were Alabama, Arkansas, Arizona, Florida, Georgia, Illinois, Louisiana, Mississippi, Missouri, Nevada, North Carolina, Oklahoma, South Carolina, Utah, and Virginia [ibid].

> "Section 1. Equality of rights under the law shall not be denied or abridged by the United States or by any state on account of sex.
>
> Section 2. The Congress shall have the power to enforce, by appropriate legislation, the provisions of this article.
>
> Section 3. This amendment shall take effect two years after the date of ratification."

On April 25, 2013 the US House of Representatives adopted a proposal to remove the end-date for the ratification of ERA. Women therefore still do not have equal rights as men in all US states.

In Sweden, however, the situation, thankfully, is different. Swedish gender equality policy is a global leader and families have the legal right to share care during maternity leave.

The girl from West Harbour in Malmö can grow up knowing that her future maternal role and gender position in Swedish society is safe. The Afghan boy, on the other hand, must learn about and embrace an entirely different world view and everyday codes than those that constitute his identity.

As I mentioned earlier, integration is a question of will and capacity to integrate. The 1980s and 1990s large immigration to Sweden ran fairly smoothly depending on the more or less common cultural background. This contrasts with today's immigration from highly contrasting cultures.

A not insignificant part of the problem is also the economic distribution policy. More and more Swedes who worked all their life are at risk to becoming poor pensioners, while asylum seekers are allowed to cost large sums. This is absolutely not fair. People who built the country should not have to feel anxious about the future. I suggest to scrap the contributions carousel and give all pensioners a reasonable monthly pension. This could neutralize incentives for hostility facing asylum seekers and emphasize our global responsibility. In addition, approved applicants should have knowledge of the Swedish language (which is required to become a Danish citizen) and introduce compulsory teaching of the humanities and democracy; its history, approach to social communication, the equal value and emphasize that religion belongs only to legal rights in the private sphere, and does not have a place in political decision-making.

When the two contrasting worlds of openness and introversion meet, extraordinary measures are required to achieve successful integration. It probably also requires several generations before individuals can feel integrated. Obviously, preliminary attitudes are crucial. But is it just a question of attitudes? What if there are inherited patterns of reactions and priorities, beyond a person's conscious control? What if there are instinctive reaction patterns that are governed by ancient inherited codes? This is the case in sexually deviant personalities, according to a recent groundbreaking study: some people carry genetic material which can be activated under certain circumstances.

"Sexual crimes, according to a never previously made study, are written in the genes. Brothers to sex offender are comparatively to the rest of the population, five times more likely to commit rape or assault ... About 40 percent of the risk of committing sexual offenses is genetic. The remaining 60 percent depends on personal and environmental factors, child abuse, upbringing, wealth and education ... The researchers found that half brothers of sex offenders were far less likely to perform sexual offense than full brothers, even though they had grown up in the same household, suggesting that a shared environment has little effect." [30]

This study is based on data from 21.566 men who were convicted of sexual offenses in Sweden between 1973 and 2009. The researchers from Oxford University and the Karolinska Institute suggest that fathers and brothers to sex offenders should be offered psychotherapy to teach them to respect limits and curb aggression.

Certainly, this form of human behavior is therefore

inherited. What if this also applies to other expressions of human behavior, such as the conviction that there is only one truth, as a large proportion of asylum seekers from theocratic societies of many generations are told? Such a possibility would imply that integration is much more difficult than first imagined.

Logically it should be the same for Swedes in their understanding of asylum seekers. If Swedish humanistic democracy is a "genetically" conditioned response pattern and value-based attitude, that would make it hard to understand the opposite.

However, if a certain behavior is inherited, it must reasonably have its origins somewhere. Referring to sex offenders, we should therefore try to reconstruct the genealogy of deviant sexual behavior. Is it a generic behavior in all men? As shown by the investigation, this is not so, so explanations must be sought elsewhere.

Do certain men always rape and defile women, or is it the result of cultural/historical causes? Are all males prone to commit rape, while the rate of incidents has been cut down by the process of civilization? The latter is a possibility: in reality most men are not sex offenders (see below).

I believe that the attitude of some men that women are sexual objects, subject to arbitrary oppression, is the heritage of the patriarchal development of the first civilizations, when nomadic life was abandoned in favor of permanent residence. The power structure that was shaped then favored the physically stronger men.

A related question is whether sex crimes also occurred before the introduction of patriarchy. The answer is that it probably always existed, but it is interesting to read what pre-patriarchal texts have to say about rapists.

In Sumerian society, about 4,500 years ago, we can get a picture about how potential rapists should be treated. A text describes how the goddess Inana was raped when she tired and fell asleep. She wakes up in the morning and notices what has happened. She searches for the offender, to administer justice. The perpetrator hides himself in misery and is supported by his father, but eventually Inana finds him and sentences him to death:

> "... holy Inana inspected herself closely. "Ah, who will compensate me? Ah, who will pay for what happened to me? ... "Father Enki, I should be compensated! What's more, someone should pay for what happened to me! ... Enki said "All right!" to her. He said "So be it!" to her. Šu-kale-tuda tried to make himself as tiny as possible, but the woman had found him among the mountains. ... and holy Inana spoke to Šu-kale-tuda: ""So! You shall die!" (Inana and Šu-kale-tuda: c.1.3.3). [31]

During the Sumerian era, women were also allowed to be much more active.

> "The women of former days used to take two husbands".[32]

In my book "Evolutionary ideas - a short story about why, when and how humans (by all accounts) took the wrong path"[33], I describe the paradigm shift, that took place, starting with the voice of a particularly gifted Akkadian woman, High priestess Enheduana (died c. 2250 BC), and then describe some of the most oppressive times for women up to the present time.

Throughout our world women of today still live under

serious oppression, and are subjected to great suffering by men. My thesis, drawing on the above-related research on sex offenders, that some men more than others used the oppression mechanism canonized by patriarchy, and this tendency found its way into human DNA strands where it is latent and can be activated.

The same process should then be applicable to other human behaviors exposed and expressed over many centuries.

That destructive behavior has found its way into our genome is bad news. However, if this is so, it would be equally true that good behavior is inheritable, bringing the potential for people to rise out of superstition and delusion. The "good" man could maybe replace the "wise" (sapiens) man, whose dubious wisdom quite clearly can and must be challenged. Will *Homo sapiens* be replaced by *Homo bonus* or *Homo empiri* (who has learned from human mistakes)?

We all descend from the first mother "Lucy", and we have undergone many transformations before *Homo sapiens* took over world domination and, after 190,000 years, (*Homo sapiens* first appeared about 200,000 years ago) made the earth a playground for repressive regimes. Until then, humans had lived in a respectful symbiosis with nature, albeit with great anxiety about nature's power and unpredictability.

Only 250 years ago, a new light hit Europe's horizon. The Enlightenment marked a starting point towards a better society. Paradoxically, it meant also the beginning of a new form of anxiety: *Globalizationis sollicitus*, which in the modern society is making itself more and more palpable. Old truths are not so true anymore. Populists lay snares to trap consensus, and pour inflammable solutions on to the fire of fear of globalization.

Human beings really just want to be happy. They keenly search for signals to guide them to happiness, but seem to have great difficulty in distinguishing genuine signals from the false by showing faith in the open society.

I choose to finish by paraphrasing Friedrich von Schiller (1759-1805):

Who knows people's happiness - before they can think freely? [34]

Notes

[1] Libris, onr:9876643.

[2] Lévy, Bernard-Henri , *Kriget är här*, Sydsvenskan, Malmö, 2015-11-16.

[3] https://quran.com.

[4] Al-Ansari, Abd Al-Hamid, Rotana Khalijiyya TV, 2016-06-03.

[5] http://americanhumanist.org/humanism/definitions_of_humanism

[6] http://www.dictionary.com/browse/theocracy. The concept of theocratic anti-humanism is the essentially same as Michel Foucault's post-structuralist critique of the concept of humanism, in that both have the language as implementer and identity carrier.

[7] Bible, http://www.kingjamesbibleonline.org/

[8] polisen.se, *Utsatta områden - sociala risker kollektiv förmåga och oönskade händelser.pdf*

[9] http://www.aftonbladet.se/nyheter/article19374579. ab, 2014-08-16. 2015.

[10] Ekot, Sveriges Radio, 2013-09-03.

[11] http://www.scb.se/sv_/Hitta-statistik/Artiklar/Antalet-asylsokande-okar-for-tredje-aret-i-rad/

[12] Fromkin, David, *A Peace to End All Peace: The Fall of the Ottoman Empire and the Creation of the Modern Middle East*, Holt paperbacks, 1989.

[13] http://koenraadelst.bharatvani.org/books/negaind/ch2.htm

[14] https://www.youtube.com/watch?v=g7TAAw3oQvg

[15] http://www.gp.se/nyheter/g%C3%B6teborg/polisen-g%C3%B6teborg-bland-de-st%C3%B6rsta-i-is-rekrytering-1.164427.

[16] Chalamish lecture based on two articles in *Cerebral*

CORTEX, Oxford Journals, England, *Dissociating Bottom-Up and Top-Down Mechanisms in the Cortico-Limbic System during Emotion Processing*, 2014-08-27 and *Neurotransmitters and prefrontal cortex-limbic system interactions: implications for plasticity and psychiatric disorders*, 2009-05-28.

[17] https://www.youtube.com watch?v=qY17d4ZhY8M.

[18] https://www.youtube.com/watch?v=g7TAAw3oQvg.

[19] http://luk.se/lagen.htm. Martin Luther bröt mot den katolska kyrkans kanoniska lag 1517.

[20] Fractured Lands: How the Arab World Came Apart, The New York Times, 2016-08-11.

[21] https://en.wikipedia.org/wiki/Sahih_al-Bukhari.

[22] http://lostislamichistory.com/jerusalem-and-umar-ibn-al-khattab/.

[23] European Court of Human Rights, "Annual Report 2003", (2004) pp. 5-6.

[24] British Library, *Magna Carta*, http: //www.bl.uk/treasures/magnacarta/translation/mc_trans.html.

[25] Wollstonecraft, Mary, *Försvar för kvinnans rättigheter*, 1792, Kvinnopolitiska nyckeltexter, Studentlitteratur, 1996.

[26] http://www.swedenabroad.com/sv-SE/Ambassader/Riyadh/Handel--service-till-svenska-foretag/Handel-med-Saudiarabien/

[27] http://www.systemicpeace.org/polity/polity4.htm.

[28] al-Alawi, Irfan, http://www.weeklystandard.com/blogs/wahhabi-internal-contradictions-saudi-arabia-seeks-wider-gulf-leadership_645231.html, 2012.

[29] Women History, http://womenshistory.about.com/od/equalrightsamendment/a/equal_rights_amendment_overview.htm, 2012.

[30] http://www.telegraph.co.uk/news/2016/04/06/ sex-offending-is-written-in-dna-of-some-men-oxford-university-fi/, 2015-04-09.7

[31] Black, J.A., Cunningham, G., Ebeling, J., Flücki-ger-Hawker, E., Robson, E., Taylor, J., and Zólyomi, G., *The Electronic Text Corpus of Sumerian Literature* (http://etcsl.orinst.ox.ac.uk/), Oxford, 1998–2006.

[32] Kramer, Samuel Noah, *The Sumerians*, University of Chicago Press, 1971.

[33] Conricus, Richard, *EVOLUTIONARY ideas – A short story about why, when and how humans (by all accounts) took the wrong path*, numen books, Malmö, 2011-2015.

[34] Travesti of *Vet jag min broder lycklig – innan han fått tänka?*

Images

Cover Munck, Edward, *"Skriet"*, lithograph, 1895, photo montage: Richard Conricus, 2016.

Page 11 http://www.qatartodayonline.com/the-arab-spring-revolutions-repercussions-and-the-way-for-ward/

Page 20 http://h2oreuse.blogspot.com/2011/03/ne ... -east.html och http://s1.zetaboards.com/anthroscape/ topic/5962678/1/.

Page 24 http://worldmiddleages.blogspot.co.il/p/the-early-caliphate-rashidun-caliphate.html

Page 23 https://www.loc.gov/item/95684017.

Page 35 Image from intenet without source mentioned.